THAT WHICH IS SEEN, AND THAT WHICH IS NOT SEEN

THAT WHICH IS SEEN, AND THAT WHICH IS NOT SEEN

FRÉDÉRIC BASTIAT

WORLD LIBRARY CLASSICS

BOOK INFORMATION

Published in 2010 by WLC Books.

INTRODUCTION

In the department of economy, an act, a habit, an institution, a law, gives birth not only to an effect, but to a series of effects. Of these effects, the first only is immediate; it manifests itself simultaneously with its cause — it is seen. The others unfold in succession — they are not seen: it is well for us, if they are foreseen. Between a good and a bad economist this constitutes the whole difference — the one takes account of the visible effect; the other takes account both of the effects which are seen, and also of those which it is necessary to foresee. Now this difference is enormous, for it almost always happens that when the immediate consequence is favourable, the ultimate consequences are fatal, and the converse. Hence it follows that the bad economist pursues a small present good, which will be followed by a great evil to come, while the true economist pursues a great good to come, — at the risk of a small present evil.

In fact, it is the same in the science of health, arts, and in that of morals. It often happens, that the sweeter the first fruit of a habit is, the more bitter are the consequences. Take, for example, debauchery, idleness, prodigality. When, therefore, a man absorbed in the effect which is seen has not yet learned to discern those which are not seen, he gives way to fatal habits, not only by inclination, but by calculation.

This explains the fatally grievous condition of mankind. Ignorance surrounds its cradle: then its actions are determined by their first consequences, the only ones which, in its first stage, it can see. It is only in the long run that it learns to take account of the others. It has to learn this lesson from two very different masters — experience and foresight. Experience teaches effectually, but brutally. It makes us acquainted with all the effects of an action, by causing us to feel them; and we cannot fail to finish by knowing that fire burns, if we have burned ourselves. For this rough teacher, I should like, if possible, to substitute a more gentle one. I mean Foresight. For this purpose I shall examine the consequences of certain economical phenomena, by placing in opposition to each other those which are seen, and those which are not seen.

I. THE BROKEN WINDOW

Have you ever witnessed the anger of the good shopkeeper, James B., when his careless son happened to break a square of glass? If you have been present at such a scene, you will most assuredly bear witness to the fact, that every one of the spectators, were there even thirty of them, by common consent apparently, offered the unfortunate owner this invariable consolation — "It is an ill wind that blows nobody good. Everybody must live, and what would become of the glaziers if panes of glass were never broken?"

Now, this form of condolence contains an entire theory, which it will be well to show up in this simple case, seeing that it is precisely the same as that which, unhappily, regulates the greater part of our economical institutions.

Suppose it cost six francs to repair the damage, and you say that the accident brings six francs to the glazier's trade — that it encourages that trade to the amount of six francs — I grant it; I have not a word to say against it; you reason justly. The glazier comes, performs his task, receives his six francs, rubs his hands, and, in his heart, blesses the careless child. All this is that which is seen.

But if, on the other hand, you come to the conclusion, as is too often the case, that it is a good thing to break windows, that it causes money to circulate, and that the encouragement of industry in general will be the result of it, you will oblige me to call out, "Stop there! your theory is confined to that which is seen; it takes no account of that which is not seen."

It is not seen that as our shopkeeper has spent six francs upon one thing, he cannot spend them upon another. It is not seen that if he had not had a window to replace, he would, perhaps, have replaced his old shoes, or added another book to his library. In short, he would have employed his six francs in some way, which this accident has prevented.

Let us take a view of industry in general, as affected by this circumstance. The window being broken, the glazier's trade is encouraged to the amount of six francs; this is that which is seen. If the window had not been broken, the shoemaker's trade (or some other) would have been encouraged to the amount of six francs; this is that which is not seen.

And if that which is not seen is taken into consideration, because it is a negative fact, as well as that which is seen, because it is a positive fact, it will be understood that neither industry in general, nor the sum total of national labour, is affected, whether windows are broken or not.

Now let us consider James B. himself. In the former supposition, that of the window being broken, he spends six francs, and has neither more nor less than he had before, the enjoyment of a window.

In the second, where we suppose the window not to have been broken, he would have spent six francs on shoes, and would have had at the same time the enjoyment of a pair of shoes and of a window.

Now, as James B. forms a part of society, we must come to the conclusion, that, taking it altogether, and making an estimate of its enjoyments and its labours, it has lost the value of the broken window.

When we arrive at this unexpected conclusion: "Society loses the value of things which are uselessly destroyed;" and we must assent to a maxim which will make the hair of protectionists stand on end — To break, to spoil, to waste, is not to encourage national labour; or, more briefly, "destruction is not profit."

What will you say, Monsieur Industriel — what will you say, disciples of good M. F. Chamans, who has calculated with so much precision how much trade would gain by the burning of Paris, from the number of houses it would be necessary to rebuild?

I am sorry to disturb these ingenious calculations, as far as their spirit has been introduced into our legislation; but I beg him to begin them again, by taking into the account that which is not seen, and placing it alongside of that which is seen. The reader must take care to remember that there are not two persons only, but three concerned in the little scene which I have submitted to his attention. One of them, James B., represents the consumer, reduced, by an act of destruction, to one enjoyment instead of two. Another under the title of the glazier, shows us the producer, whose trade is encouraged by the accident. The third is the shoemaker (or some other tradesman), whose labour suffers proportionably by the same cause. It is this third person who is always kept in the shade, and who, personating that which is not seen, is a necessary element of the problem. It is he who shows us how absurd it is to think we see a profit in an act of destruction. It is he who will soon teach us that it is not less absurd to see a profit in a restriction, which is, after all, nothing else than a partial destruction. Therefore, if you will only go to the root of all the arguments which are adduced in its favour, all you will find will be the paraphrase of this vulgar saying — What would become of the glaziers, if nobody ever broke windows?

II. THE DISBANDING OF TROOPS

It is the same with a people as it is with a man. If it wishes to give itself some gratification, it naturally considers whether it is worth what it costs. To a nation, security is the greatest of advantages. If, in order to obtain it, it is necessary to have an army of a hundred thousand men, I have nothing to say against it. It is an enjoyment bought by a sacrifice. Let me not be misunderstood upon the extent of my position. A member of the assembly proposes to disband a hundred thousand men, for the sake of relieving the tax-payers of a hundred millions.

If we confine ourselves to this answer — "The hundred millions of men, and these hundred millions of money, are indispensable to the national security: it is a sacrifice; but without this sacrifice, France would be torn by factions, or invaded by some foreign power," — I have nothing to object to this argument, which may be true or false in fact, but which theoretically contains nothing which militates against economy. The error begins when the sacrifice itself is said to be an advantage because it profits somebody.

Now I am very much mistaken if, the moment the author of the proposal has taken his seat, some orator will not rise and say — "Disband a hundred thousand men! do you know what you are saying? What will become of them? Where will they get a living? Don't you know that work is scarce everywhere? That every field is overstocked? Would you turn them out of doors to increase competition, and weigh upon the rate of wages? Just now, when it is a hard matter to live at all, it would be a pretty thing if the State must find bread for a hundred thousand individuals? Consider, besides, that the army consumes wine, clothing, arms — that it promotes the activity of manufactures in garrison towns — that it is, in short, the godsend of innumerable purveyors. Why, any one must tremble at the bare idea of doing away with this immense industrial movement."

This discourse, it is evident, concludes by voting the maintenance of a hundred thousand soldiers, for reasons drawn from the necessity of the service, and from economical considerations. It is these considerations only that I have to refute.

A hundred thousand men, costing the tax-payers a hundred millions of money, live and bring to the purveyors as much as a hundred millions can supply. This is that which is seen.

But, a hundred millions taken from the pockets of the tax-payers, cease to maintain these taxpayers and the purveyors, as far as a hundred minions reach. This is that which is not seen. Now make your calculations. Cast up, and tell me what profit there is for the masses?

I will tell you where the loss lies; and to simplify it, instead of speaking of a hundred thousand men and a million of money, it shall be of one man, and a thousand francs.

We will suppose that we are in the village of A. The recruiting sergeants go their round, and take off a man. The tax-gatherers go their round, and take off a thousand francs. The man and the sum of money are taken to Metz, and the latter is destined to support the former for a year without doing anything. If you consider Metz only, you are quite right; the measure is a very advantageous one: but if you look towards the village of A., you will judge very differently; for, unless you are very blind indeed, you will see that that village has lost a worker, and the thousand francs which would remunerate his labour, as well as the activity which, by the expenditure of those thousand francs, it would spread around it.

At first sight, there would seem to be some compensation. What took place at the village, now takes place at Metz, that is all. But the loss is to be estimated in this way:

At the village, a man dug and worked; he was a worker. At Metz, he turns to the right about, and to the left about; he is a soldier. The money and the circulation are the same in both cases; but in the one there were three hundred days of productive labour; in the other, there are three hundred days of unproductive labour, supposing, of course, that a part of the army is not indispensable to the public safety.

Now, suppose the disbanding to take place. You tell me there will be a surplus of a hundred thousand workers, that competition will be stimulated, and it will reduce the rate of wages. This is what you see.

But what you do not see is this. You do not see that to dismiss a hundred thousand soldiers is not to do away with a million of money, but to return it to the tax-payers. You do not see that to throw a hundred thousand workers on the market, is to throw into it, at the same moment, the hundred millions of money needed to pay for their labour; that, consequently, the same act which increases the supply of hands, increases also the demand; from which it follows, that your fear of a reduction of wages is unfounded. You do not see that, before the disbanding as well as after it, there are in the country a hundred millions of money corresponding with the hundred thousand men. That the whole difference consists in this: before the disbanding, the country gave the hundred millions to the hundred thousand men for doing nothing; and that after it, it pays them the same sum for working. You do not see, in short, that when a tax-payer gives his money either to a soldier in exchange for nothing, or to a worker in exchange for something, all the ultimate consequences of the circulation of this money are the same in the two cases; only, in the second case, the tax-payer receives something, in the former he receives nothing. The result is — a dead loss to the nation.

The sophism which I am here combating will not stand the test of progression, which is the touchstone of principles. If, when every compensation is made, and all interests are satisfied, there is a national profit in increasing the army, why not enroll under its banners the entire male population of the country?

III. TAXES

Have you ever chanced to hear it said "There is no better investment than taxes. Only see what a number of families it maintains, and consider how it reacts on industry; it is an inexhaustible stream, it is life itself."

In order to combat this doctrine, I must refer to my preceding refutation. Political economy knew well enough that its arguments were not so amusing that it could be said of them, repetitions please. It has, therefore, turned the proverb to its own use, well convinced that, in its mouth, repetitions teach.

The advantages which officials advocate are those which are seen. The benefit which accrues to the providers is still that which is seen. This blinds all eyes.

But the disadvantages which the tax-payers have to get rid of are those which are not seen. And the injury which results from it to the providers, is still that which is not seen, although this ought to be self-evident.

When an official spends for his own profit an extra hundred sous, it implies that a tax-payer spends for his profit a hundred sous less. But the expense of the official is seen, because the act is performed, while that of the tax-payer is not seen, because, alas! he is prevented from performing it.

You compare the nation, perhaps, to a parched tract of land, and the tax to a fertilizing rain. Be it so. But you ought also to ask yourself where are the sources of this rain and whether it is not the tax itself which draws away the moisture from the ground and dries it up?

Again, you ought to ask yourself whether it is possible that the soil can receive as much of this precious water by rain as it loses by evaporation?

There is one thing very certain, that when James B. counts out a hundred sous for the tax-gatherer, he receives nothing in return. Afterwards, when an official spends these hundred sous and returns them to James B., it is for an equal value of corn or labour. The final result is a loss to James B. of five francs.

It is very true that often, perhaps very often, the official performs for James B. an equivalent service. In this case there is no loss on either side; there is merely in exchange. Therefore, my arguments do not at all apply to useful functionaries. All I say is, — if you wish to create an office, prove its utility. Show that its value to James B., by the services which it performs for him, is equal to what it costs him. But, apart from this intrinsic utility, do not bring forward as an argument the benefit which it confers upon the official, his family, and his providers; do not assert that it encourages labour.

When James B. gives a hundred pence to a Government officer, for a really useful service, it is exactly the same as when he gives a hundred sous to a shoemaker for a pair of shoes.

But when James B. gives a hundred sous to a Government officer, and receives nothing for them unless it be annoyances, he might as well give them to a thief. It is nonsense to say that the Government officer will spend these hundred sous to the great profit of national labour; the thief would do the same; and so would James B., if he had not been stopped on the road by the extra-legal parasite, nor by the lawful sponger.

Let us accustom ourselves, then, to avoid judging of things by what is seen only, but to judge of them by that which is not seen.

Last year I was on the Committee of Finance, for under the constituency the members of the opposition were not systematically excluded from all the Commissions: in that the constituency acted wisely. We have heard M. Thiers say — "I have passed my life in opposing the legitimist party, and the priest party. Since the common danger has brought us together, now that I associate with them and know them, and now that we speak face to face, I have found out that they are not the monsters I used to imagine them."

Yes, distrust is exaggerated, hatred is fostered among parties who never mix; and if the majority would allow the minority to be present at the Commissions, it would perhaps be discovered that the ideas of the different sides are not so far removed from each other, and, above all, that their intentions are not so perverse as is supposed. However, last year I was on the Committee of Finance. Every time that one of our colleagues spoke of fixing at a moderate figure the maintenance of the President of the Republic, that of the ministers, and of the ambassadors, it was answered —

"For the good of the service, it is necessary to surround certain offices with splendour and dignity, as a means of attracting men of merit to them. A vast number of unfortunate persons apply to the President of the Republic, and it would be placing him in a very painful position to oblige him to be constantly refusing them. A certain style in the ministerial saloons is a part of the machinery of constitutional Governments."

Although such arguments may be controverted, they certainly deserve a serious examination. They are based upon the public interest, whether rightly estimated or not; and as far as I am concerned, I have much more respect for them than many of our Catos have, who are actuated by a narrow spirit of parsimony or of jealousy.

But what revolts the economical part of my conscience, and makes me blush for the intellectual resources of my country, is when this absurd relic of feudalism is brought forward, which it constantly is, and it is favourably received too:

"Besides, the luxury of great Government officers encourages the arts, industry, and labour. The head of the State and his ministers cannot give banquets and soirees without causing life to circulate through all the veins of the social body. To reduce their means, would starve Parisian industry, and consequently that of the whole nation."

I must beg you, gentlemen, to pay some little regard to arithmetic, at least; and not to say before the National Assembly in France, lest to its shame it should agree with you, that an addition gives a different sum, according to whether it is added up from the bottom to the top, or from the top to the bottom of the column.

For instance, I want to agree with a drainer to make a trench in my field for a hundred sous. Just as we have concluded our arrangement, the tax-gatherer comes, takes my hundred sous, and sends them to the Minister of the Interior; my bargain is at end, but the Minister will have another dish added to his table. Upon what ground will you dare to affirm that this official expense helps the national industry? Do you not see, that in this there is only a reversing of satisfaction and labour? A Minister has his table better covered, it is true, but it is just as true that an agriculturist has his field worse drained. A Parisian tavern-keeper has gained a hundred sous,I grant you; but then you must grant me that a drainer has been prevented from gaining five francs. It all comes to this, — that the official and the tavern-keeper being satisfied, is that which is seen; the field undrained, and the drainer deprived of his job, is that which is not seen. Dear me! how much trouble there is in proving that two and two make four; and if you succeed in proving it, it is said, "the thing is so plain it is quite tiresome," and they vote as if you had proved nothing at all.

IV. THEATRES AND FINE ARTS

Ought the State to support the arts?

There is certainly much to be said on both sides of this question. It may be said, in favor of the system of voting supplies for this purpose, that the arts enlarge, elevate, and harmonize the soul of a nation; that they divert it from too great an absorption in material occupations, encourage in it a love for the beautiful, and thus act favourably on its manners, customs, morals, and even on its industry. It may be asked, what would become of music in France without her Italian theatre and her Conservatoire; of the dramatic art. without her Theatre-Francais; of painting and sculpture, without our collections, galleries, and museums? It might even be asked, whether, without centralization, and consequently the support of fine arts, that exquisite taste would be developed which is the noble appendage of French labour, and which introduces its productions to the whole world? In the face of such results, would it not be the height of imprudence to renounce this moderate contribution from all her citizens, which, in fact, in the eyes of Europe, realizes their superiority and their glory?

To these and many other reasons, whose force I do not dispute, arguments no less forcible may be opposed. It might, first of all, be said, that there is a question of distributive justice in it. Does the right of the legislator extend to abridging the wages of the artisan, for the sake of adding to the profits of the artist? M. Lamartine said, "If you cease to support the theatre, where will you stop? Will you not necessarily be led to withdraw your support from your colleges, your museums, your institutes, and your libraries?" It might be answered, if you desire to support everything which is good and useful, where will you stop? Will you not necessarily be led to form a civil list for agriculture, industry, commerce, benevolence, education? Then, is it certain that government aid favours the progress of art?

This question is far from being settled, and we see very well that the theatres which prosper are those which depend upon their own resources. Moreover, if we come to higher considerations, we may observe, that wants and desires arise, the one from the other, and originate in regions which are more and more refined in proportion as the public wealth allows of their being satisfied; that Government ought not to take part in this correspondence, because in a certain condition of present fortune it could not by taxation stimulate the arts of necessity, without checking those of luxury, and thus interrupting the natural course of civilization. I may observe, that these artificial transpositions of wants, tastes, labour, and population, place the people in a precarious and dangerous position, without any solid basis.

These are some of the reasons alleged by the adversaries of State intervention in what concerns the order in which citizens think their wants and desires should be satisfied, and to which, consequently, their activity should be directed. I am, I confess, one of those who think that choice and impulse ought to come from below and not from above, from the citizen and not from the legislator; and the opposite doctrine appears to me to tend to the destruction of liberty and of human dignity.

But, by a deduction as false as it is unjust, do you know what economists are accused of? It is, that when we disapprove of Government support, we are supposed to disapprove of the thing itself whose support is discussed; and to be the enemies of every kind of activity, because we desire to see those activities, on the one hand free, and on the other seeking their own reward in themselves. Thus, if we think that the State should not interfere by taxation in religious affairs, we are atheists. If we think the State ought not to interfere by taxation in education, we are hostile to knowledge. If we say that the State ought not by taxation to give a fictitious value to land, or to any particular branch of industry, we are enemies to property and labour. If we think that the State ought not to support artists, we are barbarians who look upon the arts as useless.

Against such conclusions as these I protest with all my strength. Far from entertaining the absurd idea of doing away with religion, education, property, labour, and the arts, when we say that the State ought to protect the free development of all these kinds of human activity, without helping some of them at the expense of others, — we think, on the contrary, that all these living powers of society would develop themselves more harmoniously under the influence of liberty; and that, under such an influence no one of them would, as is now the case, be a source of trouble, of abuses, of tyranny, and disorder.

Our adversaries consider, that an activity which is neither aided by supplies, nor regulated by Government, is an activity destroyed. We think just the contrary. Their faith is in the legislator, not in mankind; ours is in mankind, not in the legislator.

Thus M. Lamartine said, "Upon this principle we must abolish the public exhibitions, which are the honour and the wealth of this country." But I would say to M. Lamartine, — According to your way of thinking, not to support is to abolish; because, setting out upon the maxim that nothing exists independently of the will of the State, you conclude that nothing lives but what the State causes to live. But I oppose to this assertion the very example which you have chosen, and beg you to remark, that the grandest and noblest of exhibitions, one which has been conceived in the most liberal and universal spirit — and I might even make use of the term humanitary, for it is no exaggeration — is the exhibition now preparing in London; the only one in which no Government is taking any part, and which is being paid for by no tax.

To return to the fine arts: there are, I repeat, many strong reasons to be brought, both for and against the system of Government assistance. The reader must see, that the especial object of this work leads me neither to explain these reasons, nor to decide in their favour, nor against them.

But M. Lamartine has advanced one argument which I cannot pass by in silence, for it is closely connected with this economic study. "The economical question, as regards theatres, is comprised in one word — labour. It matters little what is the nature of this labour; it is as fertile, as productive a labour as any other kind of labour in the nation. The theatres in France, you know, feed and salary no less than 80,000 workmen of different kinds; painters, masons, decorators, costumers, architects, &c., which constitute the very life and movement of several parts of this capital, and on this account they ought to have your sympathies." Your sympathies! say, rather, your money.

And further on he says: "The pleasures of Paris are the labour and the consumption of the provinces, and the luxuries of the rich are the wages and bread of 200,000 workmen of every description, who live by the manifold industry of the theatres on the surface of the republic, and who receive from these noble pleasures, which render France illustrious, the sustenance of their lives and the necessaries of their families and children. It is to them that you will give 60,000 francs." (Very well; very well. Great applause.) For my part I am constrained to say, "Very bad! Very bad!" Confining his opinion, of course, within the bounds of the economical question which we are discussing.

Yes, it is to the workmen of the theatres that a part, at least, of these 60,000 francs will go; a few bribes, perhaps, may be abstracted on the way. Perhaps, if we were to look a little more closely into the matter, we might find that the cake had gone another way, and that these workmen were fortunate who had come in for a few crumbs. But I will allow, for the sake of argument, that the entire sum does go to the painters, decorators, &e.

This is that which is seen. But whence does it come? This is the other side of the question, and quite as important as the former. Where do these 60,000 francs spring from? and where would they go if a vote of the Legislature did not direct them first towards the Rue Rivoli and thence towards the Rue Grenelle? This is what is not seen. Certainly, nobody will think of maintaining that the legislative vote has caused this sum to be hatched in a ballot urn; that it is a pure addition made to the national wealth; that but for this miraculous vote these 60,000 francs would have been for ever invisible and impalpable. It must be admitted that all that the majority can do, is to decide that they shall be taken from one place to be sent to another; and if they take one direction, it is only because they have been diverted from another.

This being the case, it is clear that the taxpayer, who has contributed one franc, will no longer have this franc at his own disposal. It is clear that he will be deprived of some gratification to the amount of one franc; and that the workman, whoever he may be, who would have received it from him, will be deprived of a benefit to that amount. Let us not, therefore, be led by a childish illusion into believing that the vote of the 60,000 francs may add any thing whatever to the well-being of the country, and to the national labour. It displaces enjoyments, it transposes wages — that is all.

Will it be said that for one kind of gratification, and one kind of labour, it substitutes more urgent, more moral, more reasonable gratifications and labour? I might dispute this; I might say, by taking 60,000 francs from the tax-payers, you diminish tile wages of labourers, drainers, carpenters, blacksmiths, and increase in proportion those of the singers.

There is nothing to prove that this latter class calls for more sympathy than the former. M. Lamartine does not say that it is so. He himself says, that the labour of the theatres is as fertile, as productive as any other (not more so); and this may be doubted; for the best proof that the latter is not so fertile as the former lies in this, that the other is to be called upon to assist it.

But this comparison between the value and the intrinsic merit of different kinds of labour, forms no part of my present subject. All I have to do here is to show, that if M. Lamartine and those persons who commend his line of argument have seen on one side the salaries gained by the providers of the comedians, they ought on the other to have seen the salaries lost by the providers of the taxpayers; for want of this, they have exposed themselves to ridicule by mistaking a displacement for a gain. If they were true to their doctrine, there would be no limits to their demands for Government aid; for that which is true of one franc and of 60,000 is true, under parallel circumstances, of a hundred millions of francs.

When taxes are the subject of discussion, Gentlemen, you ought to prove their utility by reasons from the root of the matter, but not by this unlucky assertion — "The public expenses support the working classes." This assertion disguises the important fact, that public expenses always supersede private expenses, and that therefore we bring a livelihood to one workman instead of another, but add nothing to the share of the working class as a whole. Your arguments are fashionable enough, but they are too absurd to be justified by anything like reason.

V. PUBLIC WORKS

Nothing is more natural than that a nation, after having assured itself that an enterprise will benefit the community, should have it executed by means of a general assessment. But I lose patience, I confess, when I hear this economic blunder advanced in support of such a project. "Besides, it will be a means of creating labour for the workmen."

The State opens a road, builds a palace, straightens a street, cuts a canal; and so gives work to certain workmen — this is what is seen: but it deprives certain other workmen of work, and this is what is not seen.

The road is begun. A thousand workmen come every morning, leave every evening, and take their wages — this is certain. If the road had not been decreed, if the supplies had not been voted, these good people would have had neither work nor salary there; this also is certain.

But is this all? does not the operation, as a whole, contain something else? At the moment when M. Dupin pronounces the emphatic words, "The Assembly has adopted," do the millions descend miraculously on a moonbeam into the coffers of MM. Fould and Bineau? In order that the evolution may be complete, as it is said, must not the State organise the receipts as well as the expenditure? must it not set its tax-gatherers and tax-payers to work, the former to gather, and the latter to pay? Study the question, now, in both its elements. While you state the destination given by the State to the millions voted, do not neglect to state also the destination which the taxpayer would have given, bat cannot now give, to the same. Then you will understand that a public enterprise is a coin with two sides. Upon one is engraved a labourer at work, with this device, that which is seen; on the other is a labourer out of work, with the device, that which is not seen.

The sophism which this work is intended to refute, is the more dangerous when applied to public works, inasmuch as it serves to justify the most wanton enterprises and extravagance. When a railroad or a bridge are of real utility, it is sufficient to mention this utility. But if it does not exist, what do they do? Recourse is had to this mystification: "We must find work for the workmen."

Accordingly, orders are given that the drains in the Champ-de-Mars be made and unmade. The great Napoleon, it is said, thought he was doing a very philanthropic work by causing ditches to be made and then filled up. He said, therefore, "What signifies the result? All we want is to see wealth spread among the labouring classes."

But let us go to the root of the matter. We are deceived by money. To demand the cooperation of all the citizens in a common work, in the form of money, is in reality to demand a concurrence in kind; for every one procures, by his own labour, the sum to which he is taxed. Now, if all the citizens were to be called together, and made to execute, in conjunction, a work useful to all, this would be easily understood; their reward would be found in the results of the work itself.

But after having called them together, if you force them to make roads which no one will pass through, palaces which no one will inhabit, and this under the pretext of finding them work, it would be absurd, and they would have a right to argue, "With this labour we have nothing to do; we prefer working on our own account."

A proceeding which consists in making the citizens cooperate in giving money but not labour, does not, in any way, alter the general results. The only thing is, that the loss would react upon all parties. By the former, those whom the State employs, escape their part of the loss, by adding it to that which their fellow-citizens have already suffered.

There is an article in our constitution which says: "Society favours and encourages the development of labour — by the establishment of public works, by the State, the departments, and the parishes, as a means of employing persons who are in want of work."

As a temporary measure, on any emergency, during a hard winter, this interference with the tax-payers may have its use. It acts in the same way as securities. It adds nothing either to labour or to wages, but it takes labour and wages from ordinary times to give them, at a loss it is true, to times of difficulty.

As a permanent, general, systematic measure, it is nothing else than a ruinous mystification, an impossibility, which shows a little excited labour which is seen, and bides a great deal of prevented labour which is not seen.

VI. INTERMEDIATES

Society is the total of the forced or voluntary services which men perform for each other; that is to say, of public services and private services.

The former, imposed and regulated by the law, which it is not always easy to change, even when it is desirable, may survive with it their own usefulness, and still preserve the name of public services, even when they are no longer services at all, but rather public annoyances. The latter belong to the sphere of the will, of individual responsibility. Every one gives and receives what he wishes, and what he can, after a debate. They have always the presumption of real utility, in exact proportion to their comparative value.

This is the reason why the former description of services so often become stationary, while the latter obey the law of progress.

While the exaggerated development of public services, by the waste of strength which it involves, fastens upon society a fatal sycophancy, it is a singular thing that several modern sects, attributing this character to free and private services, are endeavouring to transform professions into functions.

These sects violently oppose what they call *intermediates*. They would gladly suppress the capitalist, the banker, the speculator, the projector, the merchant, and the trader, accusing them of interposing between production and consumption, to extort from both, without giving either anything in return. Or rather, they would transfer to the State the work which they accomplish, for this work cannot be suppressed.

The sophism of the Socialists on this point is showing to the public what it pays to the intermediates in exchange for their services, and concealing from it what is necessary to be paid to the State. Here is the usual conflict between what is before our eyes, and what is perceptible to the mind only, between what is seen, and what is not seen.

It was at the time of the scarcity, in 1847, that the Socialist schools attempted and succeeded in popularizing their fatal theory. They knew very well that the most absurd notions have always a chance with people who are suffering; malesuada fames.

Therefore, by the help of the fine words, "trafficking in men by men, speculation on hunger, monopoly," they began to blacken commerce, and to cast a veil over its benefits.

"What can be the use," they say, "of leaving to the merchants the care of importing food from the United States and the Crimea? Why do not the State, the departments, and the towns, organize a service for provisions, and a magazine for stores? They would sell at a return price, and the people, poor things, would be exempted from the tribute which they pay to free, that is, to egotistical, individual, and anarchical commerce."

The tribute paid by the people to commerce, is that which is seen. The tribute which the people would pay to the State, or to its agents, in the Socialist system, is what is not seen.

In what does this pretended tribute, which the people pay to commerce, consist? In this: that two men render each other a mutual service, in all freedom, and under the pressure of competition and reduced prices.

When the hungry stomach is at Paris, and corn which can satisfy it is at Odessa, the suffering cannot cease till the corn is brought into contact with the stomach. There are three means by which this contact may be effected. 1st. The famished men may go themselves and fetch the corn. 2nd. They may leave this task to those to whose trade it belongs. 3rd. They may club together, and give the office in charge to public functionaries. Which of these three methods possesses the greatest advantages? In every time, in all countries, and the more free, enlightened, and experienced they are, men have voluntarily chosen the second. I confess that this is sufficient, in my opinion, to justify this choice. I cannot believe that mankind, as a whole, is deceiving itself upon a point which touches it so nearly. But let us consider the subject.

For thirty-six millions of citizens to go and fetch the corn they want from Odessa, is a manifest impossibility. The first means, then, goes for nothing. The consumers cannot act for themselves. They must, of necessity, have recourse to intermediates, officials or agents.

But, observe, that the first of these three means would be the most natural. In reality, the hungry man has to fetch his corn. It is a task which concerns himself; a service due to himself. If another person, on whatever ground, performs this service for him, takes the task upon himself, this latter has a claim upon him for a compensation. I mean by this to say that intermediates contain in themselves the principle of remuneration.

However that may be, since we must refer to what the Socialists call a parasite, I would ask, which of the two is the most exacting parasite, the merchant or the official?

Commerce (free, of course, otherwise I could not reason upon it), commerce, I say, is led by its own interests to study the seasons, to give daily statements of the state of the crops, to receive information from every part of the globe, to foresee wants, to take precautions beforehand. It has vessels always ready, correspondents everywhere; and it is its immediate interest to buy at the lowest possible price, to economize in all the details of its operations, and to attain the greatest results by the smallest efforts. It is not the French merchants only who are occupied in procuring provisions for France in time of need, and if their interest leads them irresistibly to accomplish their task at the smallest possible cost, the competition which they create amongst each other leads them no less irresistibly to cause the consumers to partake of the profits of those realized savings. The corn arrives; it is to the interest of commerce to sell it as soon as possible, so as to avoid risks, to realize its funds, and begin again the first opportunity.

Directed by the comparison of prices, it distributes food over the whole surface of the country, beginning always at the highest price, that is, where the demand is the greatest. It is impossible to imagine an organization more completely calculated to meet the interest of those who are in want; and the beauty of this organization, unperceived as it is by the Socialists, results from the very fact that it is free. It is true, the consumer is obliged to reimburse commerce for the expenses of conveyance, freight, store-room, commission, &c.; but can any system be devised, in which he who eats corn is not obliged to defray the expenses, whatever they may be, of bringing it within his reach? The remuneration for the service performed has to be paid also: but as regards its amount, this is reduced to the smallest possible sum by competition; and as regards its justice, it would be very strange if the artisans of Paris would not work for the merchants of Marseilles, when the merchants of Marseilles work for the artisans of Paris.

If, according to the Socialist invention, the State were to stand in the stead of commerce, what would happen? I should like to be informed where the saving would be to the public? Would it be in the price of purchase? Imagine the delegates of 40,000 parishes arriving at Odessa on a given day, and on the day of need; imagine the effect upon prices. Would the saving be in the expenses? Would fewer vessels be required, fewer sailors, fewer transports, fewer sloops, or would you be exempt from the payment of all these things? Would it be in the profits of the merchants? Would your officials go to Odessa for nothing? Would they travel and work on the principle of fraternity? Must they not live? must not they be paid for their time? And do you believe that these expenses would not exceed a thousand times the two or three per cent which the merchant gains, at the rate at which he is ready to treat?

And then consider the difficulty of levying so many taxes, and of dividing so much food. Think of the injustice, of the abuses inseparable for such an enterprise. Think of the responsibility which would weigh upon the Government.

The Socialists who have invented these follies, and who, in the days of distress, have introduced them into the minds of the masses, take to themselves literally the title of advanced men; and it is not without some danger that custom, that tyrant of tongues, authorizes the term, and the sentiment which it involves. Advanced! This supposes that these gentlemen can see further than the common people; that their only fault is, that they are too much in advance of their age, and if the time is not yet come for suppressing certain free services, pretended parasites, the fault is to be attributed to the public, which is in the rear of socialism. I say, from my soul and my conscience, the reverse is the truth; and I know not to what barbarous age we should have to go back, if we would find the level of Socialist knowledge on this subject. These modern sectarians incessantly oppose association to actual society. They overlook the fact, that society, under a free regulation, is a true association, far superior to any of those which proceed from their fertile imaginations.

Let me illustrate this by an example. Before a man, when he gets up in the morning, can put on a coat, ground must have been enclosed, broken up, drained, tilled, and sown with a particular kind of plant; flocks must have been fed, and have given their wool; this wool must have been spun, woven, dyed, and converted into cloth; this cloth must have been cut, sewed, and made into a garment. And this series of operations implies a number of others; it supposes the employment of instruments for ploughing, &c., sheepfolds, sheds, coal, machines, carriages, &e.

If society were not a perfectly real association, a person who wanted a coat would be reduced to the necessity of working in solitude; that is, of performing for himself the innumerable parts of this series, from the first stroke of the pickaxe to the last stitch which concludes the work. But, thanks to the sociability which is the distinguishing character of our race, these operations are distributed amongst a multitude of workers; and they are further subdivided, for the common good, to an extent that, as the consumption becomes more active, one single operation is able to support a new trade.

Then comes the division of the profits, which operates according to the contingent value which each has brought to the entire work. If this is not association, I should like to know what is.

Observe, that as no one of these workers has obtained the smallest particle of matter from nothingness, they are confined to performing for each other mutual services, and to helping each other in a common object, and that all may be considered, with respect to others, intermediates. If, for instance, in the course of the operation, the conveyance becomes important enough to occupy one person, the spinning another, the weaving another, why should the first be considered a parasite more than the other two? The conveyance must be made, must it not? Does not he who performs it, devote to it his time and trouble? and by so doing does he not spare that of his colleagues? Do these do more or other than this for him? Are they not equally dependent for remuneration, that is, for the division of the produce, upon the law of reduced price? Is it not in all liberty, for the common good, that these arrangements are entered into? What do we want with a Socialist then, who, under pretence of organizing for us, comes despotically to break up our voluntary arrangements, to check the division of labour, to substitute isolated efforts for combined ones, and to send civilization back? Is association, as I describe it here, in itself less association, because every one enters and leaves it freely, chooses his place in it, judges and bargains for himself on his own responsibility, and brings with him the spring and warrant of personal interest? That it may deserve this name, is it necessary that a pretended reformer should come and impose upon us his plan and his will, and as it were, to concentrate mankind in himself?

The more we examine these advanced schools, the more do we become convinced that there is but one thing at the root of them: ignorance proclaiming itself infallible, and claiming despotism in the name of this infallibility.

I hope the reader will excuse this digression. It may not be altogether useless, at a time when declamations, springing from St. Simonian, Phalansterian, and Icarian books, are invoking the press and the tribune, and which seriously threaten the liberty of labour and commercial transactions.

VII. RESTRICTIONS

M. Prohibant (it was not I who gave him this name, but M. Charles Dupin) devoted his time and capital to converting the ore found on his land into iron. As nature had been more lavish towards the Belgians, they furnished the French with iron cheaper than M. Prohibant, which means, that all the French, or France, could obtain a given quantity of iron with less labour by buying it of the honest Flemings; therefore, guided by their own interest, they did not fail to do so, and every day there might be seen a multitude of nail-smiths, blacksmiths, cartwrights, machinists, farriers, and labourers, going themselves, or sending intermediates, to supply themselves in Belgium. This displeased M. Prohibant exceedingly.

At first, it occurred to him to put an end to this abuse by his own efforts; it was the least he could do, for he was the only sufferer. "I will take my carbine," said he; "I will put four pistols into my belt; I will fill my cartridge box; I will gird on my sword, and go thus equipped to the frontier. There, the first blacksmith, nailsmith, farrier, machinist, or locksmith, who presents himself to do his own business and not mine, I will kill, to teach him how to live." At the moment of starting, M. Prohibant made a few reflections which calmed down his warlike ardour a little. He said to himself, "In the first place, it is not absolutely impossible that the purchasers of iron, my countrymen and enemies, should take the thing ill, and, instead of letting me kill them, should kill me instead; and then, even were I to call out all my servants, we should not be able to defend the passages. In short, this proceeding would cost me very dear; much more so than the result would be worth."

M. Prohibant was on the point of resigning himself to his sad fate, that of being only as free as the rest of the world, when a ray of light darted across his brain. He recollected that at Paris there is a great manufactory of laws. "What is a law?" said he to himself. "It is a measure to which, when once it is decreed, be it good or bad, everybody is bound to conform. For the execution of the same a public force is organized, and to constitute the said public force, men and money are drawn from the nation. If, then, I could only get the great Parisian manufactory to pass a little law, 'Belgian iron is prohibited,' I should obtain the following results: The Government would replace the few valets that I was going to send to the frontier by 20,000 of the sons of those refractory blacksmiths, farmers, artisans, machinists, locksmiths, nailsmiths, and labourers. Then, to keep these 20,000 custom-house officers in health and good humour, it would distribute amongst them 25,000,000 of francs, taken from these blacksmiths, nailsmiths, artisans, and labourers. They would guard the frontier much better; would cost me nothing; I should not be exposed to the brutality of the brokers, should sell the iron at my own price, and have the sweet satisfaction of seeing our great people shamefully mystified. That would teach them to proclaim themselves perpetually the harbingers and promoters of progress in Europe. Oh! it would be a capital joke, and deserves to be tried."

So M. Prohibant went to the law manufactory. Another time, perhaps, I shall relate the story of his underhand dealings, but now I shall merely mention his visible proceedings. He brought the following consideration before the view of the legislating gentlemen:

"Belgian iron is sold in France at ten francs, which obliges me to sell mine at the same price. I should like to sell at fifteen, but cannot do so on account of this Belgian iron, which I wish was at the bottom of the Red Sea. I beg you will make a law that no more Belgian iron shall enter France. Immediately I raise my price five francs, and these are the consequences: "For every hundred-weight of iron that I shall deliver to the public, I shall receive fifteen francs instead of ten; I shall grow rich more rapidly, extend my traffic, and employ more workmen. My workmen and I shall spend much more freely to the great advantage of our tradesmen for miles around. These latter, having more custom, will furnish more employment to trade, and activity on both sides will increase in the country. This fortunate piece of money, which you will drop into my strong-box, will, like a stone thrown into a lake, give birth to an infinite number of concentric circles."

Charmed with his discourse, delighted to learn that it is so easy to promote, by legislating, the prosperity of a people, the law-makers voted the restriction. "Talk of labour and economy," they said, "what is the use of these painful means of increasing the national wealth, when all that is wanted for this object is a Decree?"

And, in fact, the law produced all the consequences announced by M. Prohibant; the only thing was, it produced others which he had not foreseen. To do him justice, his reasoning was not false, but only incomplete. In endeavouring to obtain a privilege, he had taken cognizance of the effects which are seen, leaving in the background those which are not seen. He had pointed out only two personages, whereas there are three concerned in the affair. It is for us to supply this involuntary or premeditated omission.

It is true, the crown-piece, thus directed by law into M. Prohibant's strong-box, is advantageous to him and to those whose labour it would encourage; and if the Act had caused the crownpiece to descend from the moon, these good effects would not have been counterbalanced by any corresponding evils. Unfortunately, the mysterious piece of money does not come from the moon, but from the pocket of a blacksmith, or a nail-smith, or a cartwright, or a farrier, or a labourer, or a shipwright; in a word, from James B., who gives it now without receiving a grain more of iron than when he was paying ten francs. Thus, we can see at a glance that this very much alters the state of the case; for it is very evident that M. Prohibant's profit is compensated by James B.'s loss, and all that M. Prohibant can do with the crown-piece, for the encouragement of national labour, James B. might have done himself. The stone has only been thrown upon one part of the lake, because the law has prevented it from being thrown upon another.

Therefore, that which is not seen supersedes that which is seen, and at this point there remains, as the residue of the operation, a piece of injustice, and, sad to say, a piece of injustice perpetrated by the law!

This is not all. I have said that there is always a third person left in the background. I must now bring him forward, that he may reveal to us a second loss of five francs. Then we shall have the entire results of the transaction.

James B. is the possessor of fifteen francs, the fruit of his labour. He is now free. What does he do with his fifteen francs? He purchases some article of fashion for ten francs, and with it he pays (or the intermediate pay for him) for the hundred-weight of Belgian iron. After this he has five francs left. He does not throw them into the river, but (and this is what is not seen) he gives them to some tradesman in exchange for some enjoyment; to a bookseller, for instance, for Bossuet's "Discourse on Universal History."

Thus, as far as national labour is concerned, it is encouraged to the amount of fifteen francs, viz.: ten francs for the Paris article; five francs to the bookselling trade.

> *As to James B., he obtains for his fifteen francs two gratifications, viz.:*
> *1st. A hundred-weight of iron.*
> *2nd. A book.*

The Decree is put in force. How does it affect the condition of James B.? How does it affect the national labour?

James B. pays every centime of his five francs to M. Prohibant, and therefore is deprived of the pleasure of a book, or of some other thing of equal value. He loses five francs. This must be admitted; it cannot fail to be admitted, that when the restriction raises the price of things, the consumer loses the difference.

But, then, it is said, national labour is the gainer.

No, it is not the gainer; for, since the Act, it is no more encouraged than it was before, to the amount of fifteen francs.

The only thing is that, since the Act, the fifteen francs of James B. go to the metal trade, while, before it was put in force, they were divided between the milliner and the bookseller.

The violence used by M. Prohibant on the frontier, or that which he causes to be used by the law, may be judged very differently in a moral point of view. Some persons consider that plunder is perfectly justifiable, if only sanctioned by law. But, for myself, I cannot imagine anything more aggravating. However it may be, the economical results are the same in both cases.

Look at the thing as you will; but if you are impartial, you will see that no good can come of legal or illegal plunder. We do not deny that it affords M. Prohibant, or his trade, or, if you will, national industry, a profit of five francs. But we affirm that it causes two losses, one to James B., who pays fifteen francs where he otherwise would have paid ten; the other to national industry, which does not receive the difference. Take your choice of these two losses, and compensate with it the profit which we allow. The other will prove not the less a dead loss. Here is the moral: To take by violence is not to produce, but to destroy. Truly, if taking by violence was producing, this country of ours would be a little richer than she is.

VIII. MACHINERY

"A curse on machines! Every year, their increasing power devotes millions of workmen to pauperism, by depriving them of work, and therefore of wages and bread. A curse on machines!"

This is the cry which is raised by vulgar prejudice, and echoed in the journals.

But to curse machines, is to curse the spirit of humanity!

It puzzles me to conceive how any man can feel any satisfaction in such a doctrine.

For, if true, what is its inevitable consequence? That there is no activity, prosperity, wealth, or happiness possible for any people, except for those who are stupid and inert, and to whom God has not granted the fatal gift of knowing how to think, to observe, to combine, to invent, and to obtain the greatest results with the smallest means. On the contrary, rags, mean huts, poverty, and inanition, are the inevitable lot of every nation which seeks and finds in iron, fire, wind, electricity, magnetism, the laws of chemistry and mechanics, in a word, in the powers of nature, an assistance to its natural powers. We might as well say with Rousseau — "Every man that thinks is a depraved animal."

This is not all; if this doctrine is true, since all men think and invent, since all, from first to last, and at every moment of their existence, seek the cooperation of the powers of nature, and try to make the most of a little, by reducing either the work of their hands, or their expenses, so as to obtain the greatest possible amount of gratification with the smallest possible amount of labour, it must follow, as a matter of course, that the whole of mankind is rushing towards its decline, by the same mental aspiration towards progress, which torments each of its members.

Hence, it ought to be made known, by statistics, that the inhabitants of Lancashire, abandoning that land of machines, seek for work in Ireland, where they are unknown; and, by history, that barbarism darkens the epochs of civilization, and that civilization shines in times of ignorance and barbarism.

There is evidently in this mass of contradictions something which revolts us, and which leads us to suspect that the problem contains within it an element of solution which has not been sufficiently disengaged.

Here is the whole mystery: behind that which is seen, lies something which is not seen. I will endeavour to bring it to light. The demonstration I shall give will only be a repetition of the preceding one, for the problems are one and the same.

Men have a natural propensity to make the best bargain they can, when not prevented by an opposing force; that is, they like to obtain as much as they possibly can for their labour, whether the advantage is obtained from a foreign producer, or a skillful mechanical producer.

The theoretical objection which is made to this propensity is the same in both cases. In each case it is reproached with the apparent inactivity which it causes to labour. Now, labour rendered available, not inactive, is the very thing which determines it. And, therefore, in both cases, the same practical obstacle — force, is opposed to it also. The legislator prohibits foreign competition, and forbids mechanical competition. For what other means can exist for arresting a propensity which is natural to all men, but that of depriving them of their liberty?

In many countries, it is true, the legislator strikes at only one of these competitions, and confines himself to grumbling at the other. This only proves one thing, that is, that the legislator is inconsistent.

Harm Of False Premise

We need not be surprised at this. On a wrong road, inconsistency is inevitable; if it were not so, mankind would be sacrificed. A false principle never has been, and never will be, carried out to the end.

Now for our demonstration, which shall not be a long one.

James B. had two francs which he had gained by two workmen; but it occurs to him, that an arrangement of ropes and weights might be made which would diminish the labour by half. Thus he obtains the same advantage, saves a franc, and discharges a workman.

He discharges a workman: this is that which is seen.

And seeing this only, it is said, "See how misery attends civilization; this is the way that liberty is fatal to equality. The human mind has made a conquest, and immediately a workman is cast into the gulf of pauperism. James B. may possibly employ the two workmen, but then he will give them only half their wages for they will compete with each other, and offer themselves at the lowest price. Thus the rich are always growing richer, and the poor, poorer. Society wants remodelling." A very fine conclusion, and worthy of the preamble.

Happily, preamble and conclusion are both false, because, behind the half of the phenomenon which is seen, lies the other half which is not seen.

The franc saved by James B. is not seen, no more are the necessary effects of this saving.

Since, in consequence of his invention, James B. spends only one franc on hand labour in the pursuit of a determined advantage, another franc remains to him.

If, then, there is in the world a workman with unemployed arms, there is also in the world a capitalist with an unemployed franc. These two elements meet and combine, and it is as clear as daylight, that between the supply and demand of labour, and between the supply and demand of wages, the relation is in no way changed.

The invention and the workman paid with the first franc, now perform the work which was formerly accomplished by two workmen. The second workman, paid with the second franc, realizes a new kind of work.

What is the change, then, which has taken place? An additional national advantage has been gained; in other words, the invention is a gratuitous triumph — a gratuitous profit for mankind.

From the form which I have given to my demonstration, the following inference might be drawn: "It is the capitalist who reaps all the advantage from machinery. The working class, if it suffers only temporarily, never profits by it, since, by your own showing, they displace a portion of the national labour, without diminishing it, it is true, but also without increasing it."

I do not pretend, in this slight treatise, to answer every objection; the only end I have in view, is to combat a vulgar, widely spread, and dangerous prejudice. I want to prove, that a new machine only causes the discharge of a certain number of hands, when the remuneration which pays them as abstracted by force. These hands, and this remuneration, would combine to produce what it was impossible to produce before the invention; whence it follows that the final result is an increase of advantages for equal labour.

Who is the gainer by these additional advantages?

First, it is true, the capitalist, the inventor; the first who succeeds in using the machine; and this is the reward of his genius and his courage. In this case, as we have just seen, he effects a saving upon the expense of production, which, in whatever way it may be spent (and it always is spent), employs exactly as many hands as the machine caused to be dismissed.

But soon competition obliges him to lower his prices in proportion to the saving itself; and then it is no longer the inventor who reaps the benefit of the invention — it is the purchaser of what is produced, the consumer, the public, including the workmen; in a word, mankind.

And that which is not seen is, that the saving thus procured for all consumers creates a fund whence wages may be supplied, and which replaces that which the machine has exhausted.

Thus, to recur to the forementioned example, James B. obtains a profit by spending two francs in wages. Thanks to his invention, the hand labour costs him only one franc. So long as he sells the thing produced at the same price, he employs one workman less in producing this particular thing, and that is what is seen; but there is an additional workman employed by the franc which James B. has saved. This is that which is not seen.

When, by the natural progress of things, James B. is obliged to lower the price of the thing produced by one franc, then he no longer realizes a saving; then he has no longer a franc to dispose of, to procure for the national labour a new production; but then another gainer takes his place, and this gainer is mankind. Whoever buys the thing he has produced, pays a franc less, and necessarily adds this saving to the fund of wages; and this, again, is what is not seen.

Another solution, founded upon facts, has been given of this problem of machinery.

It was said, machinery reduces the expense of production, and lowers the price of the thing produced. The reduction of the profit causes an increase of consumption, which necessitates an increase of production, and, finally, the introduction of as many workmen, or more, after the invention as were necessary before it. As a proof of this, printing, weaving, &c., are instanced.

This demonstration is not a scientific one. It would lead us to conclude, that if the consumption of the particular production of which we are speaking remains stationary, or nearly so, machinery must injure labour. This is not the case.

Suppose that in a certain country all the people wore hats; if, by machinery, the price could be reduced half, it would not necessarily follow that the consumption would be doubled.

Would you say, that in this case a portion of the national labour had been paralyzed? Yes, according to the vulgar demonstration; but, according to mine, No; for even if not a single hat more should be bought in the country, the entire fund of wages would not be the less secure. That which failed to go to the hat-making trade would be found to have gone to the economy realized by all the consumers, and would thence serve to pay for all the labour which the machine had rendered useless, and to excite a new development of all the trades. And thus it is that things go on. I have known newspapers to cost eighty francs, now we pay forty-eight: here is a saving of thirty-two francs to the subscribers. It is not certain, or, at least, necessary, that the thirty-two francs should take the direction of the journalist trade; but it is certain, and necessary too, that if they do not take this direction they will take another. One makes use of them for taking in more newspapers; another, to get better living; another, better clothes; another, better furniture. It is thus that the trades are bound together. They form a vast whole, whose different parts communicate by secret canals; what is saved by one, profits all. It is very important for us to understand, that savings never take place at the expense of labour and wares.

IX. CREDIT

In all times, but more especially of late years, attempts have been made to extend wealth by the extension of credit.

I believe it is no exaggeration to say, that since the revolution of February, the Parisian presses have issued more than 10,000 pamphlets, crying up this solution of the social problem. The only basis, alas! of this solution, is an optical delusion — if, indeed, an optical delusion can be called a basis at all.

The first thing done is to confuse cash with produce, then paper money with cash; and from these two confusions it is pretended that a reality can be drawn.

It is absolutely necessary in this question to forget money, coin, bills, and the other instruments by means of which productions pass from hand to hand; our business is with the productions themselves, which are the real objects of the loan; for when a farmer borrows fifty francs to buy a plough, it is not, in reality, the fifty francs which are lent to him, but the plough: and when a merchant borrows 20,000 francs to purchase a house, it is not the 20,000 francs which he owes, but the house. Money only appears for the sake of facilitating the arrangements between the parties.

Peter may not be disposed to lend his plough, but James may be willing to lend his money. What does William do in this case? He borrows money of James, and with this money he buys the plough of Peter.

But, in point of fact, no one borrows money for the sake of the money itself; money is only the medium by which to obtain possession of productions. Now, it is impossible in any country to transmit from one person to another more productions than that country contains.

Whatever may be the amount of cash and of paper which is in circulation, the whole of the borrowers cannot receive more ploughs, houses, tools, and supplies of raw material, than the lenders altogether can furnish; for we must take care not to forget, that every borrower supposes a lender, and that what is once borrowed implies a loan.

This granted, what advantage is there in institutions of credit? It is, that they facilitate, between borrowers and lenders, the means of finding and treating with each other; but it is not in their power to cause an instantaneous increase of the things to be borrowed and lent. And yet they ought to be able to do so, if the aim of the reformers is to be attained, since they aspire to nothing less than to place ploughs, houses, tools, and provisions in the hands of all those who desire them.

And how do they intend to effect this?

By making the State security for the loan.

Let us try and fathom the subject, for it contains something which is seen, and also something which is not seen. We must endeavour to look at both.

We will suppose that there is but one plough in the world, and that two farmers apply for it.

Peter is the possessor of the only plough which is to be had in France; John and James wish to borrow it. John, by his honesty, his property, and good reputation, offers security. He inspires confidence; he has credit. James inspires little or no confidence. It naturally happens that Peter lends his plough to John.

But now, according to the Socialist plan, the State interferes, and says to Peter, "Lend your plough to James, I will be security for its return, and this security will be better than that of John, for he has no one to be responsible for him but himself; and I, although it is true that I have nothing, dispose of the fortune of the taxpayers, and it is with their money that, in case of need, I shall pay you the principal and interest." Consequently, Peter lends his plough to James: this is what is seen.

And the Socialists rub their hands, and say, "See how well our plan has answered. Thanks to the intervention of the State, poor James has a plough. He will no longer be obliged to dig the ground; he is on the road to make a fortune. It is a good thing for him, and an advantage to the nation as a whole."

Indeed, gentlemen, it is no such thing; it is no advantage to the nation, for there is something behind which is not seen.

It is not seen, that the plough is in the hands of James, only because it is not in those of John.

It is not seen, that if James farms instead of digging, John will be reduced to the necessity of digging instead of farming.

That, consequently, what was considered an increase of loan, is nothing but a displacement of loan. Besides, it is not seen that this displacement implies two acts of deep injustice.

It is an injustice to John, who, after having deserved and obtained credit by his honesty and activity, sees himself robbed of it.

It is an injustice to the tax-payers, who are made to pay a debt which is no concern of theirs.

Will any one say, that Government offers the same facilities to John as it does to James? But as there is only one plough to be had, two cannot be lent. The argument always maintains that, thanks to the intervention of the State, more will be borrowed than there are things to be lent; for the plough represents here the bulk of available capitals.

It is true, I have reduced the operation to the most simple expression of it, but if you submit the most complicated Government institutions of credit to the same test, you will be convinced that they can have but on result; viz., to displace credit, not to augment it. In one country, and in a given time, there is only a certain amount of capital available, and all are employed. In guaranteeing the non-payers, the State may, indeed, increase the number of borrowers, and thus raise the rate of interest (always to the prejudice of the tax-payer), but it has no power to increase the number of lenders, and the importance of the total of the loans.

There is one conclusion, however, which I would not for the world be suspected of drawing. I say, that the law ought not to favour, artificially, the power of borrowing, but I do not say that it ought not to restrain them artificially. If, in our system of mortgage, or in any other, there be obstacles to the diffusion of the application of credit, let them be got rid of; nothing can be better or more just than this. But this is all which is consistent with liberty, and it is all that any who are worthy of the name of reformers will ask.

X. ALGERIA

Here are four orators disputing for the platform. First, all the four speak at once; then they speak one after the other. What have they said? Some very fine things, certainly, about the power and the grandeur of France; about the necessity of sowing, if we would reap; about the brilliant future of our gigantic colony; about the advantage of diverting to a distance the surplus of our population, &e. &e. Magnificent pieces of eloquence, and always adorned with this conclusion: "Vote fifty millions, more or less, for making ports and roads in Algeria; for sending emigrants hither; for building houses and breaking up land. By so doing, you will relieve the French workman, encourage African labour, and give a stimulus to the commerce of Marseilles. It would be profitable every way."

Yes, it is all very true, if you take no account of the fifty millions until the moment when the State begins to spend them; if you only see where they go, and not whence they come; if you look only at the good they are to do when they come out of the tax-gatherer's bag, and not at the harm which has been done, and the good which has been prevented, by putting them into it. Yes, at this limited point of view, all is profit. The house which is built in Barbary is that which is seen; the harbour made in Barbary is that which is seen; the work caused in Barbary is what is seen; a few less hands in France is what is seen; a great stir with goods at Marseilles is still that which is seen.

But, besides all this, there is something which is not seen. The fifty millions expended by the State cannot be spent, as they otherwise would have been, by the tax-payers. It is necessary to deduct, from all the good attributed to the public expenditure which has been effected, all the harm caused by the prevention of private expense, unless we say that James B. would have done nothing with the crown that he had gained, and of which the tax had deprived him; an absurd assertion, for if he took the trouble to earn it, it was because he expected the satisfaction of using it, He would have repaired the palings in his garden, which he cannot now do, and this is that which is not seen. He would have manured his field, which now he cannot do, and this is what is not seen. He would have added another story to his cottage, which he cannot do now, and this is what is not seen. He might have increased the number of his tools, which he cannot do now, and this is what is not seen. He would have been better fed, better clothed, have given a better education to his children, and increased his daughter's marriage portion; this is what is not seen. He would have become a member of the Mutual Assistance

Society, but now he cannot; this is what is not seen. On one hand, are the enjoyments of which he has been deprived, and the means of action which have been destroyed in his hands; on the other, are the labour of the drainer, the carpenter, the smith, the tailor, the village-schoolmaster, which he would have encouraged, and which are now prevented — all this is what is not seen.

Much is hoped from the future prosperity of Algeria; be it so. But the drain to which France is being subjected ought not to be kept entirely out of sight. The commerce of Marseilles is pointed out to me; but if this is to be brought about by means of taxation, I shall always show that an equal commerce is destroyed thereby in other parts of the country. It is said, "There is an emigrant transported into Barbary; this is a relief to the population which remains in the country." I answer, "How can that be, if, in transporting this emigrant to Algiers, you also transport two or three times the capital which would have served to maintain him in France?"

The Minister of War has lately asserted, that every individual transported to Algeria has cost the State 8,000 francs. Now it is certain that these poor creatures could have lived very well in France on a capital of 4,000 francs. I ask, how is the French population relieved, when it is deprived of a man, and of the means of subsistence of two men?

The only object I have in view is to make it evident to the reader, that in every public expense, behind the apparent benefit, there is an evil which it is not so easy to discern. As far as in me lies, I would make him form a habit of seeing both, and taking account of both.

When a public expense is proposed, it ought to be examined in itself, separately from the pretended encouragement of labour which results from it, for this encouragement is a delusion. Whatever is done in this way at the public expense, private expense would have done all the same; therefore, the interest of labour is always out of the question.

It is not the object of this treatise to criticize the intrinsic merit of the public expenditure as applied to Algeria, but I cannot withhold a general observation. It is, that the presumption is always unfavourable to collective expenses by way of tax. Why? For this reason: First, justice always suffers from it in some degree. Since James B. had laboured to gain his crown, in the hope of receiving a gratification from it, it is to be regretted that the exchequer should interpose, and take from James B. this gratification, to bestow it upon another. Certainly, it behooves the exchequer, or those who regulate it, to give good reasons for this. It has been shown that the State gives a very provoking one, when it says, "With this crown I shall employ workmen"; for James B. (as soon as he sees it) will be sure to answer, "It is all very fine, but with this crown I might employ them myself."

Apart from this reason, others present themselves without disguise, by which the debate between the exchequer and poor James becomes much simplified. If the State says to him, "I take your crown to pay the gendarme, who saves you the trouble of providing for your own personal safety; for paving the street which you are passing through every day; for paying the magistrate who causes your property and your liberty to be respected; to maintain the soldier who maintains our frontiers," — James B., unless I am much mistaken, will pay for all this without hesitation. But if the State were to say to him, I take this crown that I may give you a little prize in case you cultivate your field well; or that I may teach your son something that you have no wish that he should learn; or that the Minister may add another to his score of dishes at dinner; I take it to build a cottage in Algeria, in which case I must take another crown every year to keep an emigrant in it, and another hundred to maintain a soldier to guard this emigrant, and another crown to maintain a general to guard this soldier," &c., &c., — I think I hear poor James exclaim, "This system of law is very much like a system of cheat!" The State foresees the objection, and what does it do? It jumbles all things together, and brings forward just that provoking reason which ought to have nothing whatever to do with the question. It talks of the effect of this crown upon labour; it points to the cook and purveyor of the Minister; it shows an emigrant, a soldier, and a general, living upon the crown; it shows, in fact, what is seen, and if James B. has not learned to take into the account what is not seen, James B. will be duped. And this is why I want to do all I can to impress it upon his mind, by repeating it over and over again.

As the public expenses displace labour without increasing it, a second serious presumption presents itself against them. To displace labour is to displace labourers, and to disturb the natural laws which regulate the distribution of the population over the country. If 50,000,000 fr. are allowed to remain in the possession of the taxpayers, since the tax-payers are everywhere, they encourage labour in the 40,000 parishes in France. They act like a natural tie, which keeps every one upon his native soil; they distribute themselves amongst all imaginable labourers and trades. If the State, by drawing off these 50,000,000 fr. from the citizens, accumulates them, and expends them on some given point, it attracts to this point a proportional quantity of displaced labour, a corresponding number of labourers, belonging to other parts; a fluctuating population, which is out of its place, and, I venture to say, dangerous when the fund is exhausted. Now here is the consequence (and this confirms all I have said): this feverish activity is, as it were, forced into a narrow space; it attracts the attention of all; it is what is seen. The people applaud; they are astonished at the beauty and facility of the plan, and expect to have it continued and extended. That which they do not see is, that an equal quantity of labour, which would probably be more valuable, has been paralyzed over the rest of France.

XI. FRUGALITY AND LUXURY

It is not only in the public expenditure that what is seen eclipses what is not seen. Setting aside what relates to political economy, this phenomenon leads to false reasoning. It causes nations to consider their moral and their material interests as contradictory to each other. What can be more discouraging, or more dismal?

For instance, there is not a father of a family who does not think it his duty to teach his children order, system, the habits of carefulness, of economy, and of moderation in spending money.

There is no religion which does not thunder against pomp and luxury. This is as it should be; but, on the other hand, how frequently do we hear the following remarks:

"To hoard, is to drain the veins of the people."

"The luxury of the great is the comfort of the little."

"Prodigals ruin themselves, but they enrich the State."

"It is the superfluity of the rich which makes bread for the poor."

Here, certainly, is a striking contradiction between the moral and the social idea.

How many eminent spirits, after having made the assertion, repose in peace. It is a thing I never could understand, for it seems to me that nothing can be more distressing than to discover two opposite tendencies in mankind. Why, it comes to degradation at each of the extremes: economy brings it to misery; prodigality plunges it into moral degradation. Happily, these vulgar maxims exhibit economy and luxury in a false light, taking account, as they do, of those immediate consequences which are seen, and not of the remote ones, which are not seen. Let us see if we can rectify this incomplete view of the case.

Mondor and his brother Aristus, after dividing the paternal inheritance, have each an income of 50,000 francs. Mondor practises the fashionable philanthropy. He is what is called a squanderer of money. He renews his furniture several times a year; changes his equipages every month. People talk of his ingenious contrivances to bring them sooner to an end: in short, he surpasses the fast livers of Balzac and Alexander Dumas.

Thus, everybody is singing his praises. It is, "Tell us about Mondor? Mondor for ever! He is the benefactor of the workman; a blessing to the people. It is true, he revels in dissipation; he splashes the passers-by; his own dignity and that of human nature are lowered a little; but what of that? He does good with his fortune, if not with himself. He causes money to circulate; he always sends the tradespeople away satisfied. Is not money made round that it may roll?"

Aristus has adopted a very different plan of life. If he is not an egotist, he is, at any rate, an individualist, for he considers expense, seeks only moderate and reasonable enjoyments, thinks of his children's prospects, and, in fact, he economises.

And what do people say of him? "What is the good of a rich fellow like him? He is a skinflint. There is something imposing, perhaps, in the simplicity of his life; and he is humane, too, and benevolent, and generous, but he calculates. He does not spend his income; his house is neither brilliant nor bustling. What good does he do to the paper hangers, the carriage makers, the horse dealers, and the confectioners?"

These opinions, which are fatal to morality, are founded upon what strikes the eye: the expenditure of the prodigal; and another, which is out of sight, the equal and even superior expenditure of the economist.

But things have been so admirably arranged by the Divine inventor of social order, that in this, as in everything else, political economy and morality, far from clashing, agree; and the wisdom of Aristus is not only more dignified, but still more profitable, than the folly of Mondor. And when I say profitable, I do not mean only profitable to Aristus, or even to society in general, but more profitable to the workmen themselves — to the trade of the time.

To prove it, it is only necessary to turn the mind's eye to those hidden consequences of human actions, which the bodily eye does not see.

Yes, the prodigality of Mondor has visible effects in every point of view. Everybody can see his landaus, his phaetons, his berlins, the delicate paintings on his ceilings, his rich carpets, the brilliant effects of his house. Every one knows that his horses run upon the turf. The dinners which he gives at the Hotel de Paris attract the attention of the crowds on the Boulevards; and it is said, "That is a generous man; far from saving his income, he is very likely breaking into his capital." This is what is seen.

It is not easy to see, with regard to the interest of workers, what becomes of the income of Aristus. If we were to trace it carefully, however, we should see that the whole of it, down to the last farthing, affords work to the labourers, as certainly as the fortune of Mondor. Only there is this difference: the wanton extravagance of Mondor is doomed to be constantly decreasing, and to come to an end without fail; whilst the wise expenditure of Aristus will go on increasing from year to year. And if this is the case, then, most assuredly, the public interest will be in unison with morality.

Aristus spends upon himself and his household 20,000 francs a year.

If that is not sufficient to content him, he does not deserve to be called a wise man. He is touched by the miseries which oppress the poorer classes; he thinks he is bound in conscience to afford them some relief, and therefore he devotes 10,000 francs to acts of benevolence. Amongst the merchants, the manufacturers, and the agriculturists, he has friends who are suffering under temporary difficulties; he makes himself acquainted with their situation, that he may assist them with prudence and efficiency, and to this work he devotes 10,000 francs more. Then he does not forget that he has daughters to portion, and sons for whose prospects it is his duty to provide, and therefore he considers it a duty to lay by and put out to interest 10,000 francs every year.

The following is a list of his expenses:

```
1st, Personal expenses......... 20,000 fr.
2nd, Benevolent objects........ 10,000
3rd, Offices of friendship..... 10,000
4th, Saving.................... 10,000
```

Let us examine each of these items, and we shall see that not a single farthing escapes the national labour.

1st. Personal expenses. — These, as far as work-people and tradesmen are concerned, have precisely the same effect as an equal sum spent by Mondor. This is self-evident, therefore we shall say no more about it.

2nd. Benevolent objects. — The 10,000 francs devoted to this purpose benefit trade in an equal degree; they reach the butcher, the baker, the tailor, and the carpenter. The only thing is, that the bread, the meat, and the clothing are not used by Aristus, but by those whom he has made his substitutes. Now, this simple substitution of one consumer for another, in no way effects trade in general. It is all one, whether Aristus spends a crown, or desires some unfortunate person to spend it instead.

3rd. Offices of friendship. — The friend to whom Aristus lends or gives 10,000 francs, does not receive them to bury them; that would be against the hypothesis. He uses them to pay for goods, or to discharge debts. In the first case, trade is encouraged. Will any one pretend to say that it gains more by Mondor's purchase of a thoroughbred horse for 10,000 francs, than by the purchase of 10,000 francs' worth of stuffs by Aristus or his friend? For, if this sum serves to pay a debt, a third person appears, viz. the creditor, who will certainly employ them upon something in his trade, his household, or his farm. He forms another medium between Aristus and the workmen. The names only are changed, the expense remains, and also the encouragement to trade.

4th. Saving. — There remains now the 10,000 francs saved; and it is here, as regards the encouragement to the arts, to trade, labour, and the workmen, that Mondor appears far superior to Aristus, although, in a moral point of view, Aristus shows himself, in some degree, superior to Mondor.

I can never look at these apparent contradictions between the great laws of nature, without a feeling of physical uneasiness which amounts to suffering. Were mankind reduced to the necessity of choosing between two parties, one of whom injures his interest, and the other his conscience, we should have nothing to hope from the future. Happily, this is not the case; and to see Aristus regain his economical superiority, as well as his moral superiority, it is sufficient to understand this consoling maxim, which is no less true from having a paradoxical appearance, "To save, is to spend."

What is Aristus's object in saving 10,000 francs? Is it to bury them in his garden? No, certainly; he intends to increase his capital and his income; consequently, this money, instead of being employed upon his own personal gratification, is used for buying land, a house, &c., or it is placed in the hands of a merchant or a banker. Follow the progress of this money in any one of these cases, and you will be convinced, that through the medium of vendors or lenders, it is encouraging labour quite as certainly as if Aristus, following the example of his brother, had exchanged it for furniture, jewels, and horses.

For when Aristus buys lands or rents for 10,000 francs, he is determined by the consideration that he does not want to spend this money. This is why you complain of him.

But, at the same time, the man who sells the land or the rent, is determined by the consideration that he does want to spend the 10,000 francs in some way; so that the money is spent in any case, either by Aristus, or by others in his stead.

With respect to the working class, to the encouragement of labour, there is only one difference between the conduct of Aristus and that of Mondor. Mondor spends the money himself and therefore the effect is seen. Aristus, spending it partly through intermediate parties, and at a distance, the effect is not seen. But, in fact, those who know how to attribute effects to their proper causes, will perceive, that what is not seen is as certain as what is seen. This is proved by the fact, that in both cases the money circulates, and does not lie in the iron chest of the wise mall, any more than it does in that of the spendthrift. It is, therefore, false to say that economy does actual harm to trade; as described above, it is equally beneficial with luxury.

But how far superior is it, if, instead of confining our thoughts to the present moment, we let them embrace a longer period!

Ten years pass away. What is become of Mondor and his fortune, and his great popularity? Mondor is ruined. Instead of spending 60,000 francs every year in the social body, he is, perhaps, a burden to it. In any case, he is no longer the delight of shopkeepers; he is no longer the patron of the arts and of trade; he is no longer of any use to the workmen, nor are his successors, whom he has brought to want.

At the end of the same ten years, Aristus not only continues to throw his income into circulation, but he adds an increasing sum from year to year to his expenses. He enlarges the national capital, that is, the fund which supplies wages, and as it is upon the extent of this fund that the demand for hands depends, he assists in progressively increasing the remuneration of the working class; and if he dies, he leaves children whom he has taught to succeed him in this work of progress and civilization.

In a moral point of view, the superiority of frugality over luxury is indisputable. It is consoling to think that it is so in political economy, to every one who, not confining his views to the immediate effects of phenomena, knows how to extend his investigations to their final effects.

XII. HAVING A RIGHT TO WORK, HAVING A RIGHT TO PROFIT

"Brethren, you must club together to find me work at your own price." This is the right to work; i.e., elementary socialism of the first degree.

"Brethren, you must club together to find me work at my own price." This is the right to profit; i.e., refined socialism, or socialism of the second degree.

Both of these live upon such of their effects as are seen. They will die by means of those effects which are not seen.

That which is seen, is the labour and the profit excited by social combination. That which is not seen, is the labour and the profit to which this same combination would give rise, if it were left to the tax-payers.

In 1848, the right to labour for a moment showed two faces. This was sufficient to ruin it in public opinion.

One of these faces was called national workshops. The other, forty-five centimes. Millions of francs went daily from the Rue Rivoli to the national workshops. This was the fair side of the medal.

And this is the reverse. If millions are taken out of a cashbox, they must first have been put into it. This is why the organizers of the right to public labour apply to the tax-payers.

Now, the peasants said, "I must pay forty-five centimes; then I must deprive myself of some clothing. I cannot manure my field; I cannot repair my house."

And the country workmen said, "As our townsman deprives himself of same clothing, there will be less work for the tailor; as he does not improve his field, there will be less work for the drainer; as he does not repair his house, there will be less work for the carpenter and mason."

It was then proved that two kinds of meal cannot come out of one sack, and that the work furnished by the Government was done at the expense of labour, paid for by the tax-payer. This was the death of the right to labour, which showed itself as much a chimera as an injustice. And yet, the right to profit, which is only an exaggeration of the right to labour, is still alive and flourishing.

Ought not the protectionist to blush at the part he would make society play?

He says to it, "You must give me work, and, more than that, lucrative work. I have foolishly fixed upon a trade by which I lose ten per cent. If you impose a tax of twenty francs upon my countrymen, and give it to me, I shall be a gainer instead of a loser. Now, profit is my right; you owe it me." Now, any society which would listen to this sophist, burden itself with taxes to satisfy him, and not perceive that the loss to which any trade is exposed is no less a loss when others are forced to make up for it, such a society, I say, would deserve the burden inflicted upon it.

Thus we learn, by the numerous subjects which I have treated, that, to be ignorant of political economy is to allow ourselves to be dazzled by the immediate effect of a phenomenon; to be acquainted with it is to embrace in thought and in forethought the whole compass of effects.

I might subject a host of other questions to the same test; but I shrink from the monotony of a constantly uniform demonstration, and I conclude by applying to political economy what Chateaubriand says of history:

"There are," he says, "two consequences in history; an immediate one, which is instantly recognized, and one in the distance, which is not at first perceived. These consequences often contradict each other; the former are the results of our own limited wisdom, the latter, those of that wisdom which endures. The providential event appears after the human event. God rises up behind men. Deny, if you will, the supreme counsel; disown its action; dispute about words; designate, by the term, force of circumstances, or reason, what the vulgar call Providence; but look to the end of an accomplished fact, and you will see that it has always produced the contrary of what was expected from it, if it was not established at first upon morality and justice."

— Chateaubriand's *Posthumous Memoirs.*

Made in United States
North Haven, CT
04 November 2026

21770212R00030